The
CAT in
the
Picture

Written by: Barbara and Jane Brackman
Cover and Book Design: Christine Mercer Kraft
Published by: Sirius Press
PMB 123, 3115 W. 6th Street, Suite C
Lawrence, Kansas 66049
siriuspress@earthlink.net

No acknowledgement of gratitude is sufficient
to thank the long ago families who loved their
cats enough to take photographs of them. Most
images in this book are from the authors'
collections of discarded snapshots found in
cardboard boxes on thrift store shelves.
Attempts have been made to correctly credit
the images, but with little success. If you see a
familiar face please contact us at Sirius Press.
We'd love to talk to the family who knows
about the cat in the picture.

Brackman, Barbara and Jane
The Cat in the Picture
ISBN 0-9721532-1-7

Printed in the United States
10 9 8 7 6 5 4 3 2 1

The CAT in the Picture

Dedicated to:
Chuck, Butch, Puddles, Houdini, Zumi, Holly, Rainier,
Tommy, Birdie, Krizia, Lilly, Boy Kitty (Udo),
Roo, Ned and Jack

By Barbara and Jane Brackman
Design by Christine Mercer Kraft

MAMMOTH
CAVE. KY.
NOVEMBER 2 1916

This page:
Photographs often speak for themselves. We can't do much to interpret beyond noting that the date is November 2, 1916, and the stalactites and owl are made of paper. Perhaps the burro, the cat and the woman are employees of a photo booth for souvenir pictures.

Cat People

"He was kind, tender, and affectionate to his children, very, very. Lincoln, I think, had no dog, had cats." [1]

Abraham Lincoln indeed was a cat person. He "was fond of dumb animals, especially cats. I have seen him fondle one for an hour," wrote a man who knew him.[2] His wife Mary referred to cats as his "hobby," his pleasure. The Union President

Left: Velvet was a cat cherished enough to warrant a formal studio portrait in 1893 in Hartford, Connecticut.

Photo: Courtesy of Michelle Holcom

shared that pleasure with Confederate General Robert E. Lee. While riding off to fight the Civil War, Lee's letters to his wife expressed concern for the house cats after the family was routed from their home in Arlington, Virginia.

Other cat people include politicians Adlai Stevenson and Theodore Roosevelt and writers Raymond Chandler and William Burroughs. We find references to the bond between people and cats in the earliest American diaries, long before the invention of the photographs we've collected for this book.

Cat people often write of the cat's virtues, their grace or their playfulness. Mark Twain wrote about one of the kittens in his cat Tammany's latest litter, who liked "to be crammed into a corner-pocket of the billiard table—-which he fits as snugly as does a finger in a glove and then he . . . spoils many a shot by putting out his paw and changing the direction of a passing ball."³ For many, the cat's aloofness is an attraction. Raymond Chandler preferred cats as pets because he thought dogs needed too much entertaining.

This little book is a companion to our first book *The Dog in The Picture,* in which we selected illustrations from several hundred pictures in our collection. We had fewer cat photos from which to choose. The reason may have nothing to do with the relative popularity of one pet over the other, but rather the elemental problems in taking a cat's portrait. You'll notice that many of our pictures consist of someone holding a cat for the camera. Cats rarely condescend to pose. But on the other hand, professional photographer Gladys Taber thought their remote dignity made them better subjects than dogs. "Cats make exquisite photographs....

They don't keep bouncing at you to be kissed just as you get the lens adjusted."[4]

We also found fewer references to cats in diaries and letters, and often what we found had an edge to it that isn't present when people write about dogs. Cats, and especially kittens, seemed expendable. A paragraph about a cat that begins rather pleasantly sometimes ends in mayhem, as when ten-year-old Mary Trussell earnestly explained that her sister's cat has disappeared but casually reassured her, "We did not kill him."

It may be that in the past, cats were considered farm animals, mousers rather than pets. Our ancestors' attitudes were formed by the view that animals had a fundamental nature that was either bad or good. Dogs, obedient and loyal, were considered virtuous; cats, distant and devious, were believed to be the familiars of witches, animals that might steal the breath from a new born baby.

While we found some differences in people's records of their cats and their dogs, we found the similarities more important. A companion animal in the picture, whether cat or dog, reveals a good deal about people and history. The detachment of long-ago faces that stiffly stare back at us in yellowed snapshots dissolves when there is a cat in the picture.

To illustrate the relationship between people and their cats, we've paired photos and quotes because they tell a similar tale, but most often they are unrelated. A photograph from 1945 may illustrate a quote from 1790. The enduring relationship between house cat and human being resonates across the centuries in *The Cat in the Picture.*

[1] Memories of James A. Gourley, a neighbor in Springfield. Emanuel Hertz, editor, *The Hidden Lincoln* (New York: Viking Press, 1938)

[2] Maunsell Bradhurst Field, *Memories of Many Men and Some Women* (New York: Harper & Brothers, 1874) Page 313.

[3] Letter from Samuel L. Clemens, October 2, 1908. Jean-Claude Suares and Seymour Chwast, *The Literary Cat* (New York: Push Pin Press, 1977) Page 104.

[4] Gladys Taber, *Ladies Home Journal,* October 1941, quoted in Edward F. Murphy, *The Crown Treasury of Relevant Quotations* (New York: Crown, 1978) Page 121.

1875

"Next to his wife and children, I verily believe my father loved his cats. One or two would commonly be seen sitting on his table—-sometimes on his shoulder. . . . On the back of an old letter there is scribbled....

Jerry, my cat
What the deuce are you at?"

Richard Henry Stoddard,
Personal Reminiscences (New York: Scribner, Armstrong & Co., 1875) Page 142.

"[A neighbor] prided himself in the size and beauty of his five cats. What pleased him most, was to stand at his door, with his thumbs in his vest-pockets, witnessing their wonderful exploits. Such were his exalted ideas of his feline pets, that he pronounced them to be far superior, both in physical and mental endowments, to all the hairy quadrupeds in creation. . . . He talked to them in Dutch, firmly believing they digested every word of it."

Francis Butler, *Dogo-graphy. The Life and Adventures of the Celebrated Dog Tiger* (New York: By the author, 1856) Page 92.

a better one than the last. Greeting from
our garden + ourselves + **cats**.
but pardon blots! - not a good
surface. Our thanks for your card M P B
                                    S G P.

13

There are cat people, and then there are those who are not, for example Mary Todd Lincoln's stepmother.

Lexington, Kentucky
May, 1848

"My dear husband,
Dear boy, I must tell you a story.
In his wanderings today [Bobby]
came across in a yard, a little kitten,
your hobby….[Eddy] was a
delighted little creature over it,
in the midst of his happiness Ma
came in. She you must know dis-
likes the whole cat race. I thought
in a very unfeeling manner, she
ordered the servant near, to throw
it out…She never appeared to
mind his screams."

Letter from Mary Todd Lincoln to
Abraham Lincoln.

David Herbert Donald, *Lincoln at Home* (New
York: Simon and Schuster, 1999) Page 660.

Boston,
Massachusetts
June 16, 1871

"I am just ready to swear! That detestable woman, Miss Tucker, rushed upon poor Toby to put him out of the dining room; I seized her; she shoo'd; he fled. . . . Papa and Mama came down upon me and shut me up, as if I had been swearing; and I forthwith drew into my shell and maintained a stony silence during dinner, while I inwardly boiled with wrath. So Miss Tucker is to insult me and my cat at pleasure, is she?"

Diary of Alice Stone Blackwell,
about 14 years old

Marlene Deahl Merrill, editor. *Growing Up in Boston's Gilded Age: The Journal of Alice Stone Blackwell*, 1872-1874. (New Haven: Yale University Press, 1990) Page 84.

New London, New Hampshire
December 19, 1860

"Dear Sister Delia,
Your kitty Gray is well,
we gave him away about a
fortnight ago but he has not
gone to his new home yet &
I guess never will. Mr. Fowler
where he was going isent very
fond of cats."

Letter from Mary Trussell
(about 10 years old) to Delia Page

Thomas Dublin, editor. *Farm to Factory:*
Women's Letters, 1830-1860 (New York:
Columbia University Press, 1981) Page 178.

Cats often adopt human families rather than the other way around.

Philadelphia, Pennsylvania
November 5, 1794

"A very pretty female Cat, intruded herself upon us this evening. We did not make her welcome at first, but she seem'd to insist on staying. Sall then gave her milk, and very soon after, she caught a poor little mouse and is now laying on the corner of my apron by the fireside as familiarly as if she had lived with us seven years."

Diary of Elizabeth Sandwith Drinker

Sarah Blank Dine, et.al., editors. *Diary of Elizabeth Drinker* (Boston: Northeastern University Press, 1991) Page 615.

And once in the house, they rule the home.

Boston, Massachusetts
September 2, 1849

"I here stop [writing] to turn the cat, who is roasting before the fire, and who though she has not quite sense enough to move when she gets too hot, is yet able to 'mullagatorny' for me to come and turn her."

Susan Hale's letter to her brother

Caroline P. Atkinson, editor.
Letters of Susan Hale (Boston: Marshall Jones Company, 1921) Page 3.

**Cats who move in at their own pleasure
sometimes leave at their leisure.**

New London, New Hampshire
December 5, 1859

"Dear Delia,
I attend school this winter; Mr. Colby
keeps; I like him very much, he aint
much cross. . . . Your Kitty Gray ran
away about three weeks ago; we none of
us know where he went (perhaps he
went after you.)
From your affeccinate
Sister Mary
P.S. I thought I would write and tell you
some more about Kitty Gray; he went
away before the snow came. We suppose
he found a good home which he liked
and so did not return, we did not kill
him."

Letter from ten-year-old Mary Trussell
to her foster sister

Thomas Dublin, editor. *Farm to Factory:
Women's Letters,* 1830-1860 (New York:
Columbia University Press, 1981)
Pages 142-143.

Jackson, Mississippi
1864

Memories of Susan Dabney
Smedes' childhood during the Civil
War when the family fled invading
Union soldiers, traveling to Jackson
with all their possessions:
"Even the pet cat. . . . On her
arrival [she] promptly run away. A
reward of twenty dollars, offered
through the morning paper, had
brought her back. When somebody
laughed at the advertisement and
thought it a joke, papa answered. . . .
'I offer it in earnest. My daughter is
a refugee and has little enough to
amuse her, and shall not lose the
kitten if I can help it.' "

Susan Dabney Smedes, *Memorials of a
Southern Planter* (Baltimore: Cushings &
Bailey, 1888) Page 221.

"For some weeks past we have had with us on the sea-shore a beautiful little Virginian girl. . . who has a remarkable fondness for a pretty black and white kitten, belonging to the house. All day long she will have her pet in her arms, talking to her when she thinks nobody is near—telling her every thing— charging her to keep some story to herself, as it is a very great secret."

Grace Greenwood, *History of My Pets* (Boston: Ticknor, Reed and Fields, 1851) Page 15.

Osborne County, Kansas
October 14, 1872

"Ma and I husked corn. . . . I
killed a rattlesnake with six
rattles. . . . We have two of the
nicest kittens that ever lived."

Diary of Luna Warner, age 17

Venola Lewis Bivans, editor. "The Diary of
Luna E. Warner, a Kansas Teenager of the Early
1870s," *Kansas Historical Quarterly,* Autumn
and Winter, 1969. Page 429.

May true friends
be around you!

J. Neuhauser

Keeping a cat in the house usually meant keeping fleas as well.

Warrenton, Virginia
1862

"September 10. A kitten followed me up and down till I began to feel a little regard for it.

September 14. My kitten is a great trial.

October 6. Last night as the previous one Charles got up twice to hunt fleas—-in consequence all the cats are banished, and my room has been thoroughly cleaned."

Diary of Margaret Nourse

Edward D. C. Campbell, Jr., editor. "Strangers and Pilgrims: The Diary of Margaret Tilloston Kemble Nourse." *Virginia Magazine of History and Biography,* Volume 91, Number 4. October, 1983. Page 498.

To become part of the family, cats often have to tolerate indignities such as the family dog.

Georgia
August 5, 1850

"Your dog Rex comes regularly at meal times; we talk to him of his master, and he gets many pieces of bread and meat for

your sake, although your sister
has sometimes to scold him for
interfering with the kittens."

Letter from Mary Jones to sons at college

Robert Manson Myers, editor. *A Georgian at
Princeton* (New York: Harcourt, Brace,
Jovanovich, 1976) Page 64.

1851

Memories of Keturah, or Kitty for short:
"I made her a little cloak, cap and bonnet and she would sit up straight, dressed in them, on a little chair, for all the world like some queer old woman. Once... I made her a gay suit of clothes, and taught her to ride my brother's little dog."

Grace Greenwood, *History of My Pets* (Boston: Ticknor, Reed and Fields, 1851) Page 4.

Norfolk, Virginia

January 26, 1863

"I miss the sweet prattling and playing of dear Wallace and Cornelius. . . .The sitting room is always in order now. Everything is still in the house. Even the old cat can lie all day on the rug without having her tail pulled."

Diary of Elizabeth Wallace

Eleanor P. Cross and Charles B. Cross, Jr., editors. *Glencoe Diary: The War Time Journal of Elizabeth Curtis Wallace* (Chesapeake, Virginia: Norfolk County Historical Society, 1968) Page 90

People love to endow cats with human characteristics.

1852

"It should be known that those who spend several hours a day in dressing, preparatory to placing themselves on a cushion, or some elevation where they may be seen, are generally

pleasant in society, but in private life ill tempered and ill-tongued. The cat and those who resemble her are no exceptions to this general rule."

James W. Redfield, *Comparative Physiognomy or Resemblances Between Men and Animals* (New York: By the Author, 1852) Page 29.

"Someone said that cats are the furthest animal from the human model. It depends upon what breed of humans you are referring to. . . ."

William S. Burroughs, *The Cat Inside* (New York: Viking, 1992) Page 51.

Many believed that cats could
predict the future.

Marshall County, Kansas
About 1960
"When a cat washes its face it
means company is coming."

Virginia Griswold, interviewed about folk customs and superstitions

S. J. Sackett and William E. Koch. *Kansas Folklore* (Lincoln: University of Nebraska Press, 1961) Page 76.

Maryland
About 1920

"If four persons shake a cat in a new quilt, whoever is standing at the corner where the cat jumps out will be married within the year."

Annie Weston Whitney and Caroline Canfield Bullock, *Folklore From Maryland* (New York: American Folklore Society, 1925) Page 557.

One cat finds another, and then two cats become many.

Osawatomie, Kansas
February 28, 1860

"Frank and Robbie want to send word to Aunt Jennie that their black cat has got eight little black kittens!! And want to know if she wouldn't call that a stack of black cats."

Letter to her sister from Sarah Everett

"Letters of John and Sarah Everett," *Kansas Historical Quarterly,* Volume 8, 1939. Page 359.

Cats keep up their end of the human-feline relationship by bringing home the latest catch to share.

Boston, Massachusetts
May 8, 1871

"I . . . found a little green snake that Toby [the cat] had brought in sprawling on the floor, and Annie holding up her skirts in the furthest corner of the kitchen watching Toby poke it about. I got the broom and swept it out, refusing to kill it, to her great wrath. Afterward I was scared by thinking Toby had swallowed it alive."

Diary of Alice Stone Blackwell, age 14

Marlene Deahl Merrill, editor. *Growing Up in Boston's Gilded Age: The Journal of Alice Stone Blackwell,* 1872-1874. (New Haven: Yale University Press, 1990) Page 71.

The hunt makes the meal tastier.

1874
"My dear Selima,
If you were to feast
every day upon
roasted partridges,
from off Dresden
china, and dip
your whiskers in
syllabubs and
creams, it could
never give you
such true enjoy-
ment as the com-
monest food procured by the
labor of your own paws."

A letter of advice written from a cat to her
kitten, in the hand of Anna Letitia Barbauld,
Memoir, Letters and a Selection from the Poems
(Boston: J.R. Osgood, 1874) Page 454.

Berrian Springs, Michigan
May 30, 1880

"It is rainy and disagreeable to day.
Friday, Neppa got into my room
and ate my dear little canary. At
least I suppose he ate it, for the
cage was tipped over and the bird
gone when I went into the room.

June 1
My little bird is not lost after all
but is down to Aunt Hattie's. If the
cat did tip the cage over, the bird
must have got out of the window.
He went down to Aunt Hattie's and
flew on her bird cage and she
caught it and I am so glad."

Dairy of Adeline Graham, Age 15
The editors guess Aunt Hattie
bought a new canary.

Janet L. Coryell and Robert C. Myers, editors.
*Adeline and Julia: Growing Up in Michigan and
On the Kansas Frontier* (East Lansing:
Michigan State University Press, 2000)
Pages 17-18.

South Dakota
About 1910

"[Brother Chall] has a little dog named 'Scoop,' and a dove. . . has adopted our place for a home. Chall always refers to her as the 'Dove 'o Peace.' The dove and dog play together, but the cat seems to feel too dignified to join the sport. I solemnly swear that some day Boss will forget his dignity and then instead of 'dove o' peace,' Chall will have scarcely a piece of dove."

Letter from Bess Corey

Philip L. Gerber, editor, *Bachelor Bess: the Homesteading Letters of Elizabeth Corey, 1909-1919* (Iowa City: University of Iowa Press, 1990) Page 326.

Springfield, Illinois
April 23, 1949

"I cannot agree that it should be the declared public policy of Illinois that a cat visiting a neighbor's yard or crossing the highways is a public nuisance. It is the nature of cats to do a certain amount of unescorted roaming. . . . The problem of cat versus bird is as old as time. If we attempt to resolve it by legislation who knows but what we may be called upon to take sides as well in the age old problems of dog versus cat, bird versus bird, or even bird versus worm."

Veto from Governor Adlai E. Stevenson

Walter Johnson, editor, *The Papers of Adlai E. Stevenson,* (Boston: Little Brown, 1973. Volume 3), Pages 73-74.

Fort Brown, Texas
March, 1857

Letter from Robert E. Lee, telling of the passing of a cat named Jim Nooks:

"I foretold his end. Coffee cream for breakfast. Pound cake for lunch. Fretted oysters for dinner. Buttered toast for tea, and mice and rats taken raw for supper. . . . Cat nature could not stand so much luxury. He grew enormously and ended in a spasm. His beauty could not save him."

Paul C. Nagel. *The Lees of Virginia: Seven Generations of an American Family* (New York: Oxford University Press, 1990) Page 255.

Like other pets, cats die too early. The lucky ones may earn an impressive obituary.

Keswick
May 18, 1833
"Alas! Grosvenor, this day poor old Rumpel was found dead, after as long and happy a life as cat could wish for, if cats form wishes on that subject. His full titles were: The most Noble the Archduke Rumpelstiltzchen, Marquis Macbum, Earl Tomlemagne, Baron Raticide, Waowhler and Skaratch. There should be court mourning in Catland."

Letter from Charles C. Southey to a friend

The Life and Correspondence of Charles C. Southey (New York: Harper & Brothers, 1851) Page 517.